HIP-HOP
Biographies

BEYONCÉ

SADDLEBACK
EDUCATIONAL PUBLISHING

HIP-HOP Biographies

Beyoncé

Chris Brown

Sean Combs

Drake

Dr. Dre

50 Cent

Jay Z

Nicki Minaj

Pharrell

Pitbull

Rihanna

Usher

Lil Wayne

Kanye West

SADDLEBACK
EDUCATIONAL PUBLISHING
www.sdlback.com

ISBN-13: 978-1-62250-927-0
ISBN-10: 1-62250-927-7
eBook: 978-1-63078-049-4

Printed in Singapore by Craft Print International Ltd
0000/CA00000000
19 18 17 16 15   1 2 3 4 5

Table of Contents

Timeline

1981: Beyoncé is born on September 4th, in Houston, Texas.

1988: Beyoncé wins her first talent show.

1990: Beyoncé joins Girls Tyme.

1996: The girls sign with Columbia Records and rename themselves "Destiny's Child."

1998: Destiny's Child releases their first album, and "No, No, No" is a hit single.

1999: Destiny's Child releases their second album, *The Writing's on the Wall*. Matthew Knowles gets into a legal feud with LeToya Luckett and LaTavia Roberson.

2000: LeToya and LaTavia are fired and replaced. Destiny's Child becomes a trio with Beyoncé, Kelly Rowland, and Michelle Williams.

2001: Destiny's Child releases *Survivor*, their third album.

2001–2003: Beyoncé stars in *Carmen: A Hip-Hopera, Austin Powers in Goldmember*, and *The Fighting Temptations*.

2003: Beyoncé releases her first solo album, *Dangerously in Love*, and begins dating Jay Z.

2004: Destiny's Child releases their fourth and final album, *Destiny Fulfilled*.

2006: Beyoncé and her mother start a clothing line, House of Deréon.

2006: Beyoncé stars in *Dreamgirls* and releases her second solo album, *B'Day*.

2008: Beyoncé marries longtime beau, Jay Z, on April 4th. She also returns to acting, playing Etta James in *Cadillac Records*. She releases her third solo album, *I Am… Sasha Fierce*.

2009: Beyoncé stars in *Obsessed*.

2010: Beyoncé makes history by taking home six Grammys in one night.

2011: Beyoncé releases her fourth solo album, *4. Billboard* magazine names Beyoncé Artist of the Millennium.

2012: Beyoncé and Jay Z welcome their daughter, Blue Ivy, to the world on January 7th.

2013: Beyoncé releases her visual album, *Beyoncé*.

2014: Beyoncé teams up with Jay Z for the "On the Run" tour.

A Natural-Born Performer

Beyoncé has been a star for nearly two *decades* She is known as a singer, dancer, and trendsetter. Beyoncé has sung for presidents and performed around the world. She has shattered records for the number of awards she has won. But at heart, she is a Southern girl. She calls Texas home. In Houston, where Beyoncé grew up, she was a shy little girl. Her parents did everything possible to see her big dreams come true.

Beyoncé is not a stage name. She was born Beyoncé Giselle Knowles on September 4, 1981. She was the first child of Tina and Matthew Knowles. They chose the name Beyoncé in honor of Tina's mother, Agnèz Deréon Beyincé.

Tina was a salon stylist. Matthew had a successful career at Xerox. He sold medical equipment. Beyoncé saw her parents triumph in business. Tina and Matthew made a very comfortable life for themselves. They went to church on Sundays. They lived in Houston's Third Ward, an upscale neighborhood. They drove nice cars. The family would often sing around the piano.

Tina and Matthew first fell in love because of music. When they were dating, they learned they had both sung in high school talent shows. Although they were not professional musicians, Tina and Matthew both loved music and gave Beyoncé important skills for her career. Beyoncé went to her first concert when she was just five years old.

She saw the legend Michael Jackson perform live. She says that was the moment she decided she wanted to be an entertainer.

When she was four years old, Beyoncé welcomed a little sister. Growing up, Solange was the more outgoing sister. Beyoncé was shy around other kids. She was very quiet. But that wouldn't hold her back.

Michael Jackson was a big influence on Beyoncé when she was a child. Later in her career, she honored him with a tribute.

Tina and Matthew never imagined that one day their little girl would be an international superstar. While she loved to dance at home, Beyoncé was not outgoing. According to her parents, she would try to make herself invisible when she walked into a room. Beyoncé was quiet in school. She says she never quite fit in with her classmates. Her parents put her in dance classes so she could break out of her shell.

Her dance teacher, Darlette Johnson, encouraged Beyoncé to perform at a school talent show. Beyoncé sang a song by John Lennon called "Imagine." The song asks people to imagine a world of peace and freedom. On stage, Beyoncé was no longer a shy and quiet girl. She blossomed in the spotlight. Beyoncé was confident and charming, and the audience loved her. She took first place in the show.

Beyoncé once said that when she steps out onto the stage, she "can be as fabulous" as she wants to be. She gets to live out her fantasies.

Tina and Matthew made every effort to nurture Beyoncé's talent. They put her in vocal classes. Beyoncé also sang in the choir at St. John's United Methodist Church. She brought down the house with her Sunday *solos*.

For a short period of time, Beyoncé went to a performing arts school. But Beyoncé felt the school was not letting her progress fast enough. Her schedule of *rehearsing* and performing came first. She worked with a private high school tutor. Beyoncé trained like an athlete. She continued taking dance classes. She practiced nonstop.

Beyoncé had the support of her whole family, including her younger sister, Solange.

Beyoncé and her friends used Tina's salon as their private stage. They would sing for ladies who were there to get their hair done. The ladies weren't there for a concert. But the girls demanded attention.

When she was nine years old, Beyoncé and her friends formed the group Girls Tyme. They were an all-girls group who sang R&B songs with hip-hop flavor. The girls in Girls Tyme were in the second and third grades. Beyoncé's best friend, Kelly Rowland, was in the group. Kelly even moved into the Knowleses' house house for a while. They had extra space, and Kelly's mom had a live-in nanny job out of town. So Beyoncé and Kelly were like sisters.

Beyoncé's friend LaTavia Roberson was also in the group. Beyoncé was the lead singer. The other girls sang backup and rapped. The group studied videos of the greats to perfect their style. They watched videos of Michael Jackson, the Supremes, and En Vogue. They made videos of themselves to play back and critique. With hard work, their dance moves and harmonies were tight.

In 1992, Beyoncé thought Girls Tyme had gotten their big break. They were going to perform on *Star Search*, a popular talent show on television. Wearing bright neon-colored jackets and jean shorts, the girls danced and sang with all their might. Beyoncé even had a solo where she rocked the crowd. But Girls Tyme lost. The girls were devastated. Beyoncé says that was the first time she had failed at something she really wanted to win. The next day, Matthew took the girls to Disneyland. He wanted to cheer them up.

Beyoncé and Kelly started together in Girls Tyme and continued together in Destiny's Child.

A Destiny Fulfilled

According to Matthew, the contestants who lost on *Star Search* were more likely to become successful than the winners. That's because the ones who lost were motivated to make changes and work harder. And that's exactly what happened.

Matthew quit his job at Xerox to focus all of his attention on managing Girls Tyme. He increased the number of hours they practiced. The girls worked on singing and dancing. They also practiced giving interviews and walking in high heels. Matthew decided that Girls Tyme would perform one show per week during the school year and two shows per week in the summer. Beyonce's friend LeToya Luckett joined the group.

Breaking into the music industry is difficult. It takes more than hard work and talent. It also takes some luck. So Matthew was taking a big risk. The family would have to rely on Tina's income alone. It was a big change in their lifestyle.

Tina had to work long hours. This put a strain on their marriage. She felt Matthew was more devoted to the group than to their marriage. She sold their home and moved into an apartment with Beyoncé, Solange, and Kelly.

Matthew took courses in artist management at Houston Community College. He started his own management company called World Music Entertainment. Matthew modeled his management style after Berry Gordy, the man who started Motown Records.

Gordy was responsible for launching the careers of classic R&B artists like the Supremes and the Temptations. Gordy groomed his artists. Each had a unique style. He treated his company like a family.

Matthew managed Beyoncé's career for years. In 2003, he sold World Music Entertainment for $10 million. It turns out that taking a risk was the right thing to do.

Matthew Knowles worked hard to make his daughter's dreams of stardom come true.

After six months apart, Matthew rejoined his family. Meanwhile, Girls Tyme was down to four members: Beyoncé, Kelly, LaTavia, and LeToya. Three of the original members were gone.

In 1996, the group was ready for a name change. They were older. They were young ladies now, not girls. They turned to the Bible for inspiration. They chose the name "Destiny's Child." It came from a passage in the Book of Isiah.

The first record company to sign Destiny's Child was Elektra Records. But Elektra dropped them. Another record company, Columbia, scooped the group up. Columbia had major artists like Mariah Carey and Michael Jackson on their label. It was a big deal!

Destiny's Child's first recording was the song "Killing Time" for the film *Men in Black*. The movie, with Will Smith and Tommy Lee Jones, was a huge hit. The group immediately went to work on their first album. It was self-titled *Destiny's Child*. Beyoncé wrote three songs on the album.

Destiny's Child didn't sell a lot right away. Radio and television were slow to catch on to the new girl group. The remix of their song "No, No, No" by Wyclef Jean was a dance hit. He called the girls "young Supremes" in one verse. He hit the nail on the head. Destiny's Child was the Supremes of a new generation.

Destiny's Child won three Soul Train Lady of Soul Awards in 1998. The group had broken through.

"No, No, No," a song from the first Destiny's Child album became a hit thanks to Wyclef Jean's remix.

Destiny's Child won three Soul Train Lady of Soul Awards in 1998.

Once Destiny's Child began selling records, everyone in Beyoncé's family shared in the success. Tina became the ladies' full-time stylist. Solange sang backup during live shows. And Matthew continued to manage the group.

The group was ready to go back to the studio and make a second record. Beyoncé wanted to take the music in a different direction. Looking back, she says their first album tried to be "too mature." The young women did not have the life experience to match what they were singing about. She believes this may be why the album wasn't an even bigger hit.

Destiny's Child named their second album *The Writing's on the Wall*. Beyoncé helped write 10 songs on the album. She was really coming into her own as a songwriter. *The Writing's on the Wall* had four singles. Each one touched on themes women could relate to. The ladies of Destiny's Child were expressing themselves with confidence.

Beyoncé was using the stories she heard at her mother's hair salon in her song writing. In fact, the video for "Bills, Bills, Bills" takes place in a salon. *The Writing's on the Wall* was extremely successful. "Bills, Bills, Bills" stayed on the charts longer than any other song in 1999. The album sold millions around the world in places like the United Kingdom, the Philippines, and Australia.

In 1999, Destiny's Child went on tour with TLC to support their new album. At the time, TLC was at the top of their game. They had just released *FanMail* with the hit songs "Unpretty" and "No Scrubs." Destiny's Child got amazing exposure from the tour. And they learned a lot as an opening act for the more experienced group.

17

Trouble in Paradise

Also in 1999, the ladies of Destiny's Child were getting ready to shoot their next video for "Say My Name." It was going to be a big, expensive production. But there was trouble. LaTavia Roberson and LeToya Luckett announced to MTV that they no longer wanted Matthew Knowles to manage the group. They said that they had no hard feelings toward Beyoncé and Kelly. They still wanted to perform in Destiny's Child. But they claimed that Matthew favored Beyoncé and Kelly. LaTavia and LeToya wanted more input.

Matthew had to think quickly. Canceling the video would waste all the money he had already spent. Matthew decided to replace LaTavia and LeToya for the video. So he found two other girls.

Michelle Williams had been working as a backup singer for another performer. Farrah Franklin had been in the video for "Bills, Bills, Bills." Michelle and Farrah substituted for LaTavia and LeToya in the video, and they did a great job. Michelle and Farrah

lip-synced the words and did the dance steps meant for the other girls. They looked like they belonged.

LaTavia and LeToya were shocked. They found out they had been replaced when they saw the video premiere on BET. Nobody had told them. They filed a lawsuit against Matthew Knowles. LaTavia and LeToya accused Matthew of nepotism and greed.

The lawsuit went public. Many fans blamed Beyoncé and Matthew for what happened. The controversy was news, and it got people talking about Destiny's Child. Even though the publicity was negative, it helped the album sell.

Beyoncé and Kelly (in the middle) would remain the heart of Destiny's Child.

Beyoncé, Kelly, and Michelle became a trio. And that was the last change made to the group.

Beyoncé was depressed about how she was portrayed in the media. The story made her look like a spoiled diva. She was also sad about losing two close friends. The four girls had grown up together. They were supposed to be celebrating the success that they had all worked so hard to achieve. But the lawsuit ended that.

In 2000, Matthew fired LaTavia and LeToya. The lawsuit was settled out of court. Both sides agreed they would not make any negative comments about each other.

Beyoncé and Kelly had to move on quickly. They were in the public spotlight. And Destiny's Child had a full schedule of performances. The show had to go on. Michelle and Farrah became members of the group. The new group gave interviews, toured, and rehearsed together. They had to live and breathe their work. But Farrah could not keep up with the demanding schedule. After just a few months and missing concerts and events, she was let go. Destiny's Child had become a trio. Beyoncé, Kelly, and Michelle were determined to succeed despite all the drama.

Beyoncé poured her feelings into her next song, "Independent Women Part 1." This time Beyoncé didn't need to draw on the experience of the women from her mother's salon. She had earned this experience on her own.

"Independent Women Part 1" was included on the soundtrack to the movie *Charlie's Angels.* The video features Beyoncé, Kelly, and Michelle as the Angels. The ladies sang about being independent, strong, and determined. The video was a statement to all the haters. Beyoncé and Destiny's Child proclaimed that they would continue to rise and meet every challenge they might face. It was a message a lot of women could relate to. That song reached the top of the charts and stayed there for 11 straight weeks.

Beyoncé the Survivor

Outwardly, Beyoncé may have appeared confident. Inside, she was worried. The group once had seven members. Then it went down to four. Could they continue to have success as a trio? Would they be able to top their last hit? And would the media ever stop gossiping about their issues behind the scenes?

One radio DJ went so far as to joke that being in Destiny's Child was like being on the TV show *Survivor*. He said that each week people tuned in to see who would be voted off the island. Not everyone was laughing. Beyoncé used the joke as fuel for her fire. She wrote the song "Survivor" in response to her critics.

The songs starts, "Now that you're out of my life, I'm so much better / You thought that I'd be weak without you, but I'm stronger." It wasn't hard to see why LaTavia and LeToya thought Beyoncé might have been talking about them. It sounded to them like an attack. But Beyoncé insisted that song was addressing her haters in the media.

Destiny's Child named their 2001 album *Survivor*, and it featured Beyoncé's songwriting skills. She played a part in writing and producing every song on the album. Michelle turned out to be the perfect third member—she worked really well with Beyoncé and Kelly. She had a strong work ethic, a strong religious faith, and a voice that blended beautifully with theirs.

Survivor shot to the top of the charts around the world. The album debuted at number one in nine countries. It sold more copies in the first week than any other album in Columbia Records' history. Selling nearly eight million copies, *Survivor* was the number one album of 2001. With the help of Beyoncé's songwriting magic, the ladies of Destiny's Child not only survived, they dominated.

Beyoncé, Kelly, and Michelle were a winning formula for Destiny's Child.

Beyoncé experienced many firsts while working on *Survivor*. She had a new level of creative control in the studio. She wrote songs and arranged all the vocals. Beyoncé told a clear story on *Survivor*, something their earlier albums had failed to do. She focused on speaking to and about women.

Beyoncé has often talked about her feminist attitude. She recognizes that it can be difficult being a woman in this world. She says that she wants to write music that helps women escape their stress. But she also thinks about empowering women with her lyrics. She says that women have to define themselves, not let others define them. They need to become leaders who reach out and get what they want. She tries to represent this attitude in her music.

The single "Bootylicious" is one of those feminist anthems. Beyoncé, Kelly, and Michelle taught women to be proud of their bodies, curves and all. In 2006, the *Oxford English Dictionary* added the word *bootylicious* to the dictionary. Beyoncé had made it a household word.

The year 2001 continued to be a fabulous one for Beyoncé. Destiny's Child was invited to sing at President Bush's inauguration. The next month, they were nominated for five awards and performed at the Grammy Awards. The highlight of the year came when Beyoncé won the ASCAP Songwriter of the Year. It was a big honor. Beyoncé was the first black woman and second female in history to win the prize. Destiny's Child won a total of five awards in 2001. They were at the top.

But 2001 was also a year of tragedy. The attacks on 9/11 horrified the nation. Destiny's Child canceled their European tour. Alongside Bon Jovi, Elton John, and Paul McCartney, they performed at a benefit concert for the victims and survivors. They helped raise more than $30 million.

In 2001, Destiny's Child was on fire!

Independent Woman: Beyoncé Flies Solo

Beyoncé was ready for some new challenges. Destiny's Child decided to take to a break, and Beyoncé was interested in acting. In 2001, she starred in MTV's melodrama *Carmen: A Hip-Hopera*. Set in modern-day Philadelphia, the movie was a modern take on the classic opera *Carmen*. The cast had many hip-hop stars in it, including Mos Def, Rah Digga, Jermaine Dupri, and Da Brat. Beyoncé even had the chance to reunite with Wyclef Jean on the set. Playing the lead role of Carmen, Beyoncé rapped, sang, and danced in the TV musical.

Next, she landed a role in *Austin Powers in Goldmember*. Beyoncé says that she was nervous to make the leap to the big screen. She played a character called Foxxy Cleopatra. *Goldmember* earned over $70 million in its first weekend.

Beyoncé's acting roles got bigger and better. In the movie *Dreamgirls*, Beyoncé played the lead singer of the Dreams, a Detroit singing group loosely based on the Supremes. Beyoncé was perfect for the role. She had studied Diana Ross and the Supremes since she was a young girl. Beyoncé was nominated for a Golden Globe for Best Actress and another for Best Original Song. *Dreamgirls* was a stepping-stone to her next role.

Beyoncé's character "Foxxy Cleopatra" was based on Foxy Brown, a movie character from the 1970s.

In 2008, Beyoncé played Etta James in the movie *Cadillac Records*. Etta James was a famous blues and soul singer in the 1960s. James is perhaps most famous for the classic love song "At Last." Beyoncé felt honored to portray another one of her heroes.

Etta James struggled with drug addiction. So Beyoncé went to Phoenix House, a place where people go to get treatment for addiction. That visit helped her prepare for the role. She wanted to learn first-hand what drug abuse looked like. Beyoncé was nominated for multiple awards. She donated her salary to create a cosmetology program at Phoenix House.

For her first solo album, Beyoncé won five Grammy Awards.

While Beyoncé was busy on the movie set, Michelle and Kelly were busy in the recording studio. Michelle released her first *gospel* album, *Heart to Yours*, and it was the best-selling gospel album of the year. Kelly also released her debut, *Simply Deep*. Her song "Dilemma," featuring the rapper Nelly, was a smash. Beyoncé was ready to make some music on her own too.

For her solo effort, Beyoncé wanted full creative control. She wrote 43 songs. Of those, 15 made the final cut. She was the co-executive producer alongside her father, Matthew.

Around this time, there were rumors that Beyoncé was dating rapper Jay Z. But Beyoncé and Jay Z both denied those rumors. Beyoncé had learned early on to keep her personal life private. She had learned all about being the subject of gossip when LaTavia and LeToya were fired from Destiny's Child.

But the title of her 2003 album, *Dangerously in Love*, made people wonder even more. In addition, the video for the lead single "Crazy in Love" featured Jay Z. The *chemistry* between the two of them was obvious. "Crazy in Love" was a smash single. And the album *Dangerously in Love* was hugely successful. It stayed at number one for eight weeks and eventually sold over 10 million copies.

Beyoncé had the time of her life at the Grammy Awards that year. She won a stunning total of five Grammys! But that wasn't all. She also got to perform with Prince! He had been one of her idols since she was a child. She returned to the stage later that night to sing "Dangerously in Love."

With the success of the album and all her awards, Beyoncé was ready to take off on her "Dangerously in Love Tour."

Beyoncé, Kelly, and Michelle had proved they could be successful on their own. This wanted to come together for one final album. This time things would be different. On *Survivor*, Beyoncé had written almost every song on the album. Now, each member was ready to contribute her own lyrics and melodies. Beyoncé says that their final album, *Destiny Fulfilled*, released in 2004, started a new chapter in their lives.

Destiny Fulfilled was just as successful as their earlier albums. It sold more than four million copies around the world. Beyoncé, Michelle, and Kelly went on the "Destiny Fulfilled... and Lovin' It Tour". They traveled to more than 60 countries, performing in places like Japan and Australia. On the last night of the tour in Spain, Destiny's Child announced that they were officially parting ways. This was their last concert together.

In interviews, each member said they supported one another in the decision. This breakup was unlike the one with LaTavia and LeToya. The women were separating on friendly terms. They hoped that one day they would come back together after spreading their wings.

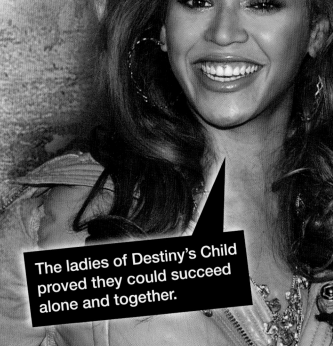

The ladies of Destiny's Child proved they could succeed alone and together.

Michelle went on to become popular gospel singer and Broadway actress. She's starred in musicals like musicals like *Fela!*, *Chicago*, and *Aida.* Her gospel records like *Heart to Yours* and *Do You Know* were bestsellers. Kelly went on to become a successful R&B singer. She's released four albums, all of which have topped the charts.

The ladies have reunited on stage just a few times since their breakup. In 2006, they performed in Houston to sing the National Anthem for the NBA finals. Their performance was electric. In 2013, they performed a medley of their hits at Super Bowl XLVII and brought down the house.

Beyoncé Takes Control of Business

The public had watched Beyoncé blossom from a girl to a woman. And her audience watched her style develop along the way. Beyoncé was known for being elegant, sexy, and *fierce* in her everyday fashion and on the red carpet. She was a style icon. It seemed natural for her to start a fashion line. And even more natural to team up with her mother, Tina.

Tina had been sewing costumes and styling hair for Beyoncé and her group since they were children. Tina had an elegant, trendy, and hip fashion sense. She had learned to sew from her own mother, Agnèz. Agnèz had worked as a seamstress in order to send Tina to a private Catholic school.

Beyoncé and Tina called their fashion line House of Deréon. The name honored Tina's mother, Agnèz Deréon Beyincé. Together, the mother-daughter team designed hip casual clothing and elegant evening gowns. Deréon sold in department stores around the country and online.

The Rock and Roll Hall of Fame considers the star's style legendary. In 2014, it opened an exhibit of Beyoncé's outfits. There, you can see the clothes she wore on the cover of *Dangerously in Love*. You can also see the outfit from her 2013 Super Bowl performance.

Beyoncé and her mother, Tina, started a fashion line called House of Deréon.

But clothing wasn't Beyoncé's only business. She has also signed advertising deals with Pepsi, Tommy Hilfiger, and L'Oreal.

Beyoncé was more than just a beautiful and talented singer and actress. She had excellent business sense. And that has made her a very wealthy woman. Between 2007 and 2008, Beyoncé made $80 million from her business *ventures*, tours, and album sales.

Beyoncé put out her next album *B'Day* in 2006. The title of the album was a celebration of her 25th birthday. Again, Beyoncé took control of the project. She arranged, wrote, and produced the album with some of the best musicians in the industry. The fusion of soul, funk, and hip-hop was inspired by her film roles (*Dreamgirls* and *Cadillac Records*) and her relationship with Jay Z.

Two singles from *B'day*, "Upgrade U" and "Déjà Vu," featured Jay Z. He was now officially her boyfriend. But the breakout hit of the album was "Irreplaceable." Beyoncé sang passionately about ending a relationship with a man who didn't appreciate her. She hired an all-female band and went on an international tour called "The Beyoncé Experience." The tour made $90 million.

Two years later, Beyoncé started work on her third album, *I Am... Sasha Fierce*. It was like two albums in one. The first side, *I Am*, was slow and personal. The second side, *Sasha Fierce*, was upbeat and funky. Beyoncé said that Jay Z and Etta James inspired her to push her artistic boundaries.

For her album *B'Day*, Beyoncé took inspiration from many places, including her role in *Dreamgirls*.

Beyoncé explained that she has always had two sides to her personality. Beyoncé was quiet and shy. Sasha Fierce was the diva who stomped around in high heels and commanded the stage. She was the alter ego who helped Beyoncé break out of her shell from the time she was a child.

I Am… Sasha Fierce debuted at number one and sold millions of copies around the world. The video for "Single Ladies (Put a Ring on It)" inspired a dance craze. Beyoncé's lyrics empowered women to demand respect and loyalty from men. Few people knew that the single was inspired by real-life events. Beyoncé and Jay Z had secretly married earlier that year. He did put a ring on it!

Beyoncé and Jay Z were able to keep their marriage plans a secret from the press.

WE Will NeVer Bé FoRGoTtEn

Beyoncé married Jay Z in a small private ceremony in New York on April 4, 2008. Somehow, they managed to keep their marriage a secret! The media only found out afterward by searching the public records.

A shared love of music drew the artists together. They both had the drive to become superstars. And they were music royalty. The King of Hip-Hop was marrying the Queen of R&B. Beyoncé says that Jay Z has taught her how to be a better woman, friend, and artist. They started dating when she was 20 years old. He helped her to be bold and take chances.

Beyoncé and Jay Z come from very different worlds. Beyoncé was raised in a middle-class suburb of Houston, Texas. Shawn Carter (Jay Z) was born and raised in the Marcy Houses in Brooklyn, New York. His neighborhood was full of poverty and crime. Crack cocaine had flooded the streets of Brooklyn in the 1980s. And Jay Z had made money selling drugs.

By the time Beyoncé started dating Jay Z, he was already a massively popular rap star with his own clothing line. He was on his way to becoming one of the wealthiest and most powerful businessmen in the music industry.

These two successful artists brought a lot of money to the marriage. They negotiated a pre-nuptial agreement. This legal contract makes sure that Beyoncé and Jay Z can protect the money they made before their marriage.

In 2008, the spotlight was also on another power couple: Barack and Michelle Obama. One of the highlights of President Obama's first inauguration was at the Neighborhood Ball. The first couple danced as Beyoncé sang "At Last." It was a song made famous by Etta James, the singer that Beyoncé had portrayed in the movie. The song expressed what many people were feeling at that moment.

Who Runs the World?

As Beyoncé's marriage was beginning, another relationship was ending. In 2011, Beyoncé asked her father to step down as her manager. It was scary to finally stand on her own and call her own shots. But she felt it would help her develop as an artist. In her documentary, *Life Is But a Dream*, Beyoncé talks about that decision. She says it was a sad and stressful time. But she felt it was the right thing to do. She wanted her dad to be a father, not a business partner.

Beyoncé took a six-month break before recording her fourth solo album. She needed to plan the direction her career would take. She also wanted to take some personal time. Beyoncé had been working hard since she was a child to make her dream happen. It was time to enjoy the success. During her break, Beyoncé went to the ballet and museums. She traveled around the world and spent time with family. She was regaining some balance in her life.

Beyoncé came back from her break refreshed. She started to record her fourth solo album, simply titled *4*. Beyoncé says she wanted to mix together everything she loved—rock, pop, funk, and R&B. It was her own musical gumbo. Out of the 72 songs Beyoncé wrote and recorded, 12 made it to the album.

In interviews, Beyoncé talks about how she creates her albums. She says that songwriting is her way of expressing her heartache and happiness. She writes from a very personal place. Music is her therapy. Fans loved the honesty and vulnerability of her new songs. Like her other albums before it, *4* debuted at number one on the music charts.

In *Life Is But a Dream*, Beyoncé opened up about her life.

Beyoncé had her daughter, Blue Ivy, on January 7, 2012.

Beyoncé and Jay Z expanded their family on January 7, 2012. Their daughter, Blue Ivy Carter, was born. Beyoncé was overjoyed. She had been waiting a long time for this moment. In interviews, Beyoncé said she felt she had a new purpose in life. She was delighted to be a mother.

Beyoncé had kept her pregnancy a secret from the public. She was terrified. Could she continue her training and performance schedule? Was it safe? Her doctor assured her that she'd be fine, so Beyoncé went on with the show. She performed at the Billboard Music Awards while pregnant. The performance was extraordinary. She sang the feminist anthem "Run the World (Girls)" in front of a huge screen that projected images she danced around. It really did look like she ran the world. Right after the performance, her mother presented her with the Billboard Millennium Award.

Soon Beyoncé wouldn't be able to keep her secret hidden any longer. Her belly was growing. She performed "Love on Top," a love song inspired by Michael Jackson. At the end of the performance, Beyoncé threw down her microphone, opened her sparkly purple jacket, and revealed her growing belly to the world. Beyoncé set a Twitter record when 8,000 tweets about her pregnancy went up every second.

After having Blue Ivy, Beyoncé began to open up more about her personal life. She released an autobiographical documentary on HBO called *Life Is But a Dream*. In it, she reveals that she had suffered a miscarriage a few years earlier. She had been devastated by the sudden loss.

In 2013, Beyoncé continued her brilliant career while juggling the demands of motherhood. In January, she delivered a powerhouse performance of the "Star Spangled Banner" for President Obama's second inauguration. There was some controversy over the fact that she lip-synched the song. Beyoncé said that she just wanted the day to be perfect. She responded to critics who doubted her ability by singing the anthem perfectly at a live press conference. When she finished, she smiled and asked, "Any questions?"

In February, she performed during halftime at Super Bowl XLVII. She performed a medley of her greatest hits. Kelly and Michelle joined her for a Destiny's Child reunion! A week later, she took home a Grammy for "Love on Top."

In April of that year, she set out on the "Mrs. Carter Show" world tour, performing at packed stadiums around the world.

On December 13, 2013, Beyoncé made history again. Without any publicity, she released her fifth studio album, *Beyoncé*, over the Internet. It included 14 songs and 17 music videos! She described it as a "visual album." Beyoncé said that she recorded the album in private because she wanted to make this album's release special.

Beyoncé was highly personal. The album explored the joy and insecurity that come with marriage and motherhood. She sang that it was possible to be empowered and sexy after giving birth. Moms could be fabulous! Each music video was like a mini-movie; each told a different story. The videos were shot all over the world, including South America, Paris, Brazil, and New York.

No one knew she was recording *Beyoncé*, but the news of its release went viral overnight! It sold more than one million digital copies in less than a month. It was the fastest-selling album in iTunes Store history. No entertainer had done this before. Beyoncé set a new standard for the music industry.

Beyoncé sang at the second inauguration of President Obama.

Beyoncé tries to be a good role model for her daughter and women everywhere.

Beyoncé has reached a level of fame and fortune that few people ever reach. But she has never forgotten those who are less fortunate. Throughout her career, Beyoncé has shown generosity through philanthropy.

Beyoncé still returns to St. John's United Methodist, the Houston church where she sang as a girl. She participates in food drives and vows never to forget her hometown, the place that shaped her. She has built centers for youth and housing for the homeless in the Houston area.

In 2003, Beyoncé headlined an international charity concert. In 2005, Beyoncé and Kelly Rowland started the Survivor Foundation to help the victims of Hurricane Katrina.

After playing Etta James in *Cadillac Records*, Beyoncé opened the Beyoncé Cosmetology Center with her mother. Her program helps recovering addicts train for salon jobs. Each year, Beyoncé pledges $100,000 to help addicts make better lives for themselves. Over the years Beyoncé has also raised money for diabetes research, victims of domestic violence, and children experiencing poverty. She truly is generous with her time and fortune.

Beyoncé Knowles-Carter is a powerhouse. She is a creative soul who is original and adventurous. She is an accomplished dancer, songwriter, filmmaker, fashion designer, and actress. Throughout her career, she's been unafraid to explore new territory and reach what may seem impossible. Many people think she is the most versatile and popular African American female in American music history.

Beyoncé takes her responsibility as a role model seriously. She actively inspires girls and women to embrace their power and beauty. She reminds them that they can be independent women who run the world. But Beyoncé is not only an entertainer. She is a proud mother, wife, and friend who values family, sisterhood, and love above all else.

Vocabulary

anthem	(noun)	a song that people feel speaks for them as a group
autobiographical	(adjective)	a work that someone creates about his or her own life
chemistry	(noun)	a physical attraction between two people
cosmetology	(noun)	the study of salon styling for hair, makeup, and nails
debut	(verb)	to appear for the first time
decade	(noun)	a ten-year period of time
devastated	(adjective)	very upset
diabetes	(noun)	a disease that causes too much sugar to stay in the blood
diva	(noun)	a person who expects to get special treatment
documentary	(noun)	a movie that presents facts about a subject
empower	(verb)	to make someone feel powerful and able
exposure	(noun)	attention from the public
fierce	(adjective)	powerful and strong
fusion	(noun)	two or more things joined into one
gospel	(noun)	a type of music that is sung in church
gumbo	(noun)	a mixture
Hurricane Katrina	(noun)	a terrible storm that flooded New Orleans in 2005
inauguration	(noun)	a formal occasion when a president officially takes the job
insecurity	(noun)	a lack of confidence or self-doubt
legend	(noun)	a person who has achieved a level of fame that lasts for long time
lip-synch	(verb)	to move your lips in a way that looks like you're singing

medley	(noun)	a group of songs that are performed together
miscarriage	(noun)	a pregnancy that ends too early for the baby to survive
negotiate	(verb)	to come to an agreement through discussion
nepotism	(noun)	hiring or giving special treatment to a relative
passionately	(adverb)	with lots of energy and feeling
philanthropy	(noun)	a pattern of giving to organizations and people who need help
portray	(verb)	to act the part of someone in a movie
proclaim	(verb)	to strongly state or claim
publicity	(noun)	information that brings attention to someone or something
R&B	(noun)	a style of music with soulful singing and a strong beat. The initials stand for rhythm and blues.
rehearse	(verb)	to practice for a performance
remix	(noun)	a song that is changed in some way from the original version
solo	(noun)	performing alone
stepping-stone	(noun)	something that helps you get something you want
venture	(noun)	a project
verse	(noun)	a section of a song that comes between the repeating chorus
viral	(adjective)	spreading quickly, like a virus
vulnerability	(noun)	weakness, flaws
work ethic	(noun)	a willingness to work hard in order to succeed

Photo Credits